D1476906

A BABY BOOK for YOU

Museum of Fine Arts, Boston

A Bulfinch Press Book
Little, Brown and Company

BOSTON • NEW YORK • TORONTO • LONDON

First published in 1994 by the Museum of Fine Arts, Boston
Second printing, 1997

ISBN 0-8212-2282-1

Front cover art by Kate Greenaway
Back cover collage by Richard Kehl

Developed, designed and produced by Nan Jernigan, Mystic, Connecticut

Bulfinch Press is an imprint and trademark of Little, Brown and Company (Inc.)
Published simultaneously in Canada by Little, Brown and Company (Canada) Limited

PRINTED IN ITALY

Your Child's First Love Letter

Dear Parents,

Of all the storybooks you could ever buy, none will be more interesting to your child than the story of his or her own life. When was I born? Where did we live then? Did I like my first birthday cake? No classic fairy tale or nursery rhyme will match the story this book will tell and no other storybook will elicit the bright-eyed pride of *A Baby Book for You*. In a way, the story you create here is the first love letter your child will receive.

These are some of the ways that you can use this book.

⊗ Create Baby's own photo album. Don't worry about picking the perfect picture, but do try to include pictures of you and your child, of you and your baby sleeping, of Baby being fed, Baby in stroller, Baby with favorite toys. As mundane as these details may seem today, years from now they will fascinate you and your child and remind you both of this warm and wonderful time in your lives.

⊗ Before Baby is born, jot down names you are considering before they are forgotten, and gifts from baby showers as well as baby furniture and clothes borrowed from friends.

⊗ If you are adopting a child, you'll find a special page of celebration, entitled "The Day We Met You." Families who do not need page 16 may simply discard it.

⊗ When your child is about two, you can begin to read this book as a bedtime story. You'll find poems and nursery rhymes along with classic illustrations to supplement your baby's own story. As your baby develops more language, you can add your baby's own words as captions to photographs.

⊗ As Baby grows you can use this book together. You'll find pages for your budding little artist to add a drawing each year and to color in the growth chart.

⊗ It's hard to imagine now, but when your baby becomes a parent for the first time, you'll want to get this book out again and cherish the memories.

Contents

Some Time

Last night, my darling, as you slept,
I thought I heard you sigh,
And to your little crib I crept,
And watched a space thereby;
Then, bending down, I kissed your brow
– For, oh! I love you so –
You are too young to know it now,
But some time you shall know.

Eugene Field

We joyfully announce
the arrival of our _____

(Baby's Name) _____

(Date) _____

(Day of Week) _____ (Hour) _____ (Month) _____

(Weight) _____ (Length) _____

(Parents' Names) _____

Paste your Announcement here.

Waiting for You

I first discovered you were coming on _____

The Doctor thought you would be born on _____

(MOTHER) I first heard your heartbeat on _____

and felt you kicking on _____

(FATHER) I first heard your heartbeat on _____

and felt you kicking on _____

Our Doctor's name was _____

To prepare for your birth, we _____

_____

_____

The first people we told about your impending

arrival were _____

_____

_____

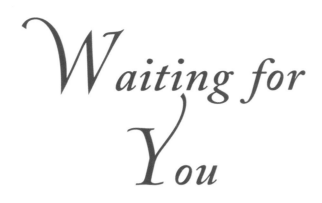

*Paste a photo of Mother and Father before Baby's birth,
or Baby's ultrasound photo, here.*

Before you were born, our nicknames for you were _____

Your Parents

Your Mother's full name is _____

and her nickname is _____

She was born on _____ in _____

When she was growing up she lived in _____

and went to school in _____ and in _____

She has _____ sisters and _____ brothers and they were born in this order:

_____

_____

Your Father's full name is _____

and his nickname is _____

He was born on _____ in _____

When he was growing up he lived in _____

and went to school in _____ and in _____

He has _____ sisters and _____ brothers and they were born in this order:

_____

_____

Your Mother and Father met on _____

in _____

When your Mother was a baby,
she looked like this.

When your Father was a baby,
he looked like this.

Who do you look like?

Paste photo of Baby here.

$\mathcal{Y}$*our*

great-grandmother

name _____

birthplace _____

birth date _____

great-grandmother

name _____

birthplace _____

birth date _____

great-grandfather

name _____

birthplace _____

birth date _____

great-grandfather

name _____

birthplace _____

birth date _____

paternal grandmother

name _____

birthplace _____

birth date _____

paternal grandfather

name _____

birthplace _____

birth date _____

Father

name _____

birthplace _____

birth date _____

Family Tree

great-grandmother

name _____

birthplace _____

birth date _____

great-grandmother

name _____

birthplace _____

birth date _____

great-grandfather

name _____

birthplace _____

birth date _____

great-grandfather

name _____

birthplace _____

birth date _____

maternal grandmother

name _____

birthplace _____

birth date _____

maternal grandfather

name _____

birthplace _____

birth date _____

Mother

name _____

birthplace _____

birth date _____

The Day You Were Born

You were born at _____ a.m./p.m. on _____

This is the story of your birth _____

_____

_____

Your were born at _____ hospital and _____

_____ helped in the delivery room.

The Doctor/Midwife's name was _____

When you were born you were:

_____   _____
(Height)   (Eye Color)

_____   _____
(Weight)   (Hair Color)

$\mathcal{P}$hoto and $\mathcal{F}$ootprint

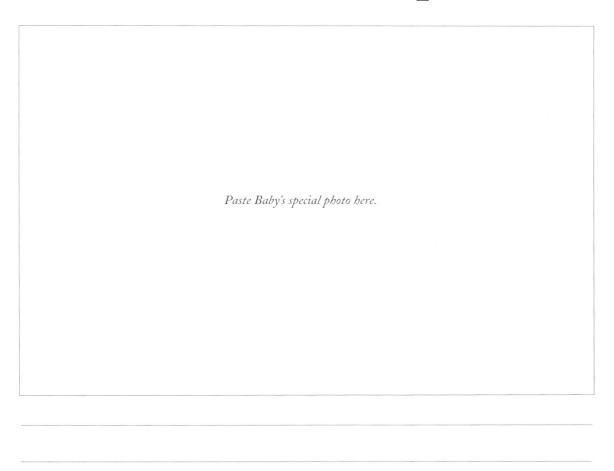

Paste Baby's special photo here.

Paste Baby's footprint here

The Day We Met You

We were first told you were coming to live with us on _____
(date)

and we were very excited because we had been waiting _____
(months, years)

to adopt you. When we first met you were _____ old

and you lived in _____

You came to live with us _____ and we travelled by

_____ to bring you home. To prepare for your arrival we

_____

This is how we felt when we first saw you: (MOTHER) _____

_____

(FATHER) _____

Not Flesh of My Flesh

Not flesh of my flesh
Nor bone of my bone,
But miraculously my own.
Never forget, even for a minute.
You weren't born under my heart,
But in it.

Author unknown

$\mathcal{P}$hoto

Paste Baby's special photo here.

Your Name

We thought a lot about your name. We read books, made lists and decided to name you

_____

Some of the other names we considered were:

❧• _Girls' names_ •❧   ❧• _Boys' names_ •❧

_____   _____

_____   _____

_____   _____

_____   _____

_____   _____

_____   _____

_____   _____

_____   _____

Pat • A • Cake

Pat-a-cake, Pat-a-cake
Baker's Man!
Bake me a cake as fast as you can.
Roll it, and pat it,
and mark it with a B,
And put it in the oven
for Baby and me.

KATE GREENAWAY

Your First Days

When you were first born, you slept _____ hours at a time. You stayed in the hospital

for _____ days and our first visitors were _____

_____

_____

_____

_____

Bringing Baby Home

We took you home on _____ at _____ o'clock. When we arrived, your

_____ were waiting there to greet you.
(grandparents, aunt, brother, or sister)

We lived at _____ and the nursery was

_____ You slept in a _____ and your room was _____
(cradle, crib) *(color)*

Paste a family photo with Baby here.

The World on the Day You Were Born

The weather was _____

The President was _____

Some important world events were _____

_____

In our town, people were talking about _____

_____

The popular movies when you were born were _____

and favorite movie stars were _____

The most popular music was _____ and we liked

to listen to _____

We were reading books by _____

and our favorite television shows were _____

_____

You were born in the _____ and the major sporting event at that time of year
                         (season)
was _____

In addition to your birth, these special events also occurred in the year you were born

_____

_____

Paste newspaper headlines here.

Your Grandparents

This is _____

Your Mother's Mother

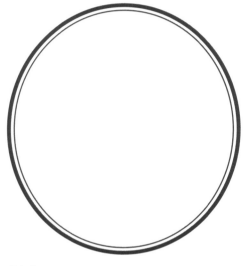

This is _____

Your Mother's Father

With Trumpet and Drum

With big tin trumpet and little red drum,
Marching like soldiers, the children come!
It's this way and that way they circle and file —
My! but that music of theirs is fine!

Your Grandparents

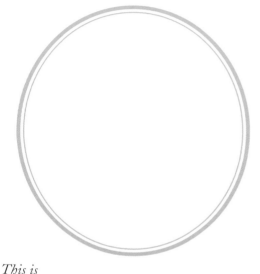

This is _____

Your Father's Mother

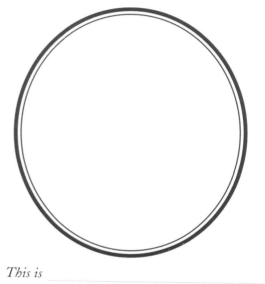

This is _____

Your Father's Father

This way and that way, and after a while
They march straight into this heart of mine!
A sturdy old heart but it has to succumb
To the blare of that trumpet and beat
of that drum!

Eugene Field

Visitors' Wishes for Baby

Gifts for You

❧• *Gift* •❧   ❧• *Giver* •❧

_____   _____

_____   _____

_____   _____

_____   _____

_____   _____

_____   _____

_____   _____

_____   _____

_____   _____

_____   _____

_____   _____

Your First
Three Months

Weight at one month _____ two months _____ three months _____

Height at one month _____ two months _____ three months _____

When you were first born you slept _____ hours at a time, and at _____ weeks old

you began to sleep _____ hours during the day. You first slept through the night at

_____ months old.

Paste photo of Baby at one month old here.

We fed you _____ and you ate about

_____ times a day and _____ at night.

You lifted your head by yourself when you were _____ weeks old and you began to

entertain us with coos and gurgles when you were _____ weeks old. You first smiled

when you were _____ weeks old, and you smiled at _____

Your first trip outside was _____

Paste photo of Baby at three months old here.

We marveled at your _____

_____

_____

Some of the songs we sang to you

were _____

_____

_____

_____

_____

Kisses for Baby

Ganderfeather's Gift

I was just a little thing
When a fairy came and kissed me;
Floating in upon the light
Of a haunted summer night,
Lo, the fairies came to sing
Pretty slumber songs and bring
Certain boons that else had missed me.
From a dream I turned to see
What those strangers brought for me,
When that fairy up and kissed me —
Here, upon this cheek, he kissed me!

Eugene Field

So, So, Rock-A-By So!

So, so, rock-a-by so!
Off to the garden where dreamikins grow;
And here is a kiss on your winkyblink eyes,
And here is a kiss on your dimpledown cheek
And here is a kiss for the treasure that lies
In the beautiful garden way up in the skies
Which you seek.
Now mind these three kisses wherever you go —
So, so, rock-a-by so!

Eugene Field

Visits to the Doctor

Doctor's Name _____

Blood Type _____

Immunizations

Type	Date	Reaction
_____	_____	_____
_____	_____	_____
_____	_____	_____
_____	_____	_____
_____	_____	_____
_____	_____	_____
_____	_____	_____
_____	_____	_____
_____	_____	_____
_____	_____	_____

Childhood Illnesses
Date

Measles _____ _____

Chicken Pox _____ _____

Mumps _____ _____

Rubella _____ _____

Ear Infection _____ _____

Ear Infection _____ _____

_____ _____

_____ _____

_____ _____

_____ _____

Allergies

_____

_____

_____

_____

_____

Accidents

_____

_____

_____

_____

_____

Your Second Three Months

Weight at four months _____ five months _____ six months _____

Height at four months _____ five months _____ six months _____

When we go out for a walk, we put you in your _____

and we go _____ Our favorite place to walk is _____

Paste photo of Baby at four, five or six months here.

You smile when you are _____ and your

favorite toy is _____

You are now eating _____

You also like to put these things in your mouth _____

You are fascinated by _____

_____

Your schedule looks like this:

Morning _____

_____

Afternoon _____

_____

Evening _____

_____

Night _____

Special Notes _____

_____

_____

_____

Hey Diddle Diddle

Hey, diddle, diddle!
The cat and the fiddle,
The cow jumped over the moon;

The little dog laughed
To see such sport,
And the dish ran away with the spoon.

Starting to Move

Activity	*Age*
You raised your head	
You turned over	
You sat up	
You pulled yourself up to a standing position	
You crawled backwards	
You crawled forwards	
You stood alone	
You took your first steps	
You ran	
You waved your hands and danced to music	

Water
Baby

When you have your bath you _____

_____

Who gives you your bath? _____

Do you like a bubble bath? _____

Some of your favorite water toys are _____

The first time you went in water outdoors you _____

_____

Your Seventh to Ninth Months

Your world is expanding and you like to reach and grab for _____

(rattle, mobile, adult glasses)

_____ Your favorite object to grasp is _____

You now enjoy eating _____ with your fingers, and you like to feed yourself

_____ with a spoon. You make us laugh when you _____

_____

_____

Photo of Baby eating, playing, or bathing.

Photo of Baby playing with friends at daycare.

Father and Baby play _____

_____

Mother and Baby play _____

_____

Other people who look after you now are _____

_____ *and with them you like to*

play _____

You like to wave good-bye to _____ *and you play peek-a-boo*

with _____

JACK & JILL.

Jack and Jill

Jack and Jill went up the hill,
To fetch a pail of water;
Jack fell down, and broke his crown,
And Jill came tumbling after.

LITTLE
BO·PEEP

WALTER CRANE

Little Bo-Peep

Little Bo-Peep has lost her sheep,
And can't tell where to find them;
Let them alone, they'll come home,
And bring their tails behind them.

x

43

First Encounters

When you first saw snow you _____

When you first saw rain you _____

When you saw your first dog you _____

When you saw your first cat you _____

On your first trip to the zoo or farm you _____

When you first recognized yourself in the

mirror you _____

Your reaction to your first taste of ice cream was

_____

Your first reaction to bubbles was _____

_____

Your first reaction to insects was _____

_____

Baby's Favorites

Your favorite blanket _____

Your favorite way to sleep _____ with your
                                    (back, stomach, side)

_____ in your mouth
    (pacifier, thumb, finger)

Your favorite toy _____

Your favorite stuffed animal _____

Your favorite song _____

Your favorite book _____

Your favorite food _____

Your favorite friend _____

Your favorite television program/video

_____

_____

_____

Your Tenth to Twelfth Months

You have now begun to move and you like to explore by _____

and now your favorite game to play with Mother is _____

and your favorite game to play with Father is _____

You make us laugh when you _____

_____

Paste photo of Baby at ten or eleven months here.

Your First Birthday

We celebrated your first birthday by _____

We invited _____

_____

Your cake was _____

At the party you most enjoyed _____

and we'll never forget _____

_____

Paste photo of Baby's first birthday party here.

The Fairies

Up the airy mountain,
    Down the rushy glen,
We daren't go a-hunting
    For fear of little men;
Wee folk, good folk,
    Trooping all together;
Green jacket, red cap,
    And white owl's feather!

Down along the rocky shore
    Some make their home,
They live on crispy pancakes
    Of yellow tide-foam;
Some in the reeds
    Of the black mountain lake,
With frogs for their watch-dogs,
    All night awake.

By the craggy hill-side,
    Through the mosses bare,
They have planted thorn-trees
    For pleasure here and there.
Is any man so daring
    As dig them up in spite,
He shall find their sharpest thorns
    In his bed at night.

Up the airy mountain,
    Down the rushy glen,
We daren't go a-hunting
    For fear of little men;
Wee folk, good folk,
    Trooping all together;
Green jacket, red cap,
    And white owl's feather!

WILLIAM ALLINGHAM

49

Baby's Firsts

༄• *Accomplishment* •༄   ༄• *Date* •༄

_____   _____

_____   _____

_____   _____

_____   _____

_____   _____

_____   _____

_____   _____

_____   _____

_____   _____

_____   _____

_____   _____

_____   _____

Baby's First Haircut

When you were _____ *months old you had your first haircut. Your baby hair was*

_____ *and* _____ *and* _____
      (color)   *(straight or curly)*

cut your hair.

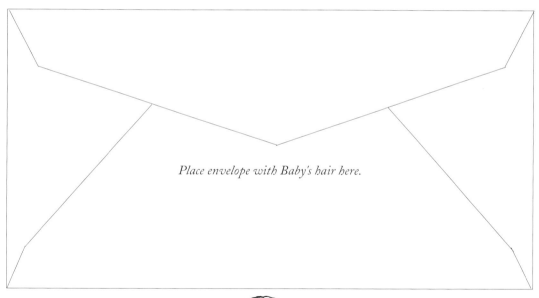

Place envelope with Baby's hair here.

KATE GREENAWAY

Your Second Year

Paste your photo at age 2 here.

Your favorite activity is _____ and your

favorite toy is _____

Your favorite playmates are _____

Other people who look after you this year are _____

_____

When you are happy you _____ and when you

are frustrated you _____

Our favorite expression of yours is _____

We celebrated your second _____ *and we went to* _____ *house.*
                                    (holiday)

The festivities included _____ *and the tradition you liked the most*

was _____

Our favorite memories of you are _____

_____

Your biggest accomplishment this year was _____

_____ *at age* _____

Drawn by _____ *on* _____

Your Third Year

Paste your photo at age 3 here.

Your favorite activity is _____ *and your*

favorite toy is _____

Your favorite playmates are _____

_____

Other people who look after you this year are _____

_____

You make us laugh when you _____

Our favorite expression of yours is _____

We celebrated your third _____ and we went to _____ house.
                              (holiday)

The festivities included _____ and the tradition you liked the most

was _____

Our favorite memories of you are _____

_____

Your biggest accomplishment this year was _____

_____ at age _____

Drawn by _____ on _____

Your Fourth Year

Paste your photo at age 4 here.

_____

Your favorite activity is _____ *and your*

favorite toy is _____

Your favorite playmates are _____

_____

Other people who look after you this year are _____

You go to nursery school at _____

and your teachers are _____

Our favorite expression of yours is _____

We celebrated your fourth _____ *and we went to* _____ *house.*
        (holiday)

The festivities included _____ *and the tradition you liked the most*

was _____

Our favorite memories of you are _____

_____

Your biggest accomplishment this year was _____

_____ *at age* _____

Drawn by _____ *on* _____

Your Fifth Year

Paste your photo at age 5 here.

_____

Your favorite activity is _____ *and your*

favorite toy is _____

Your favorite playmates are _____

_____

Other people who looked after you this year are _____

You go to school at _____

and your teachers are _____

Our favorite expression of yours is _____

We celebrated your fifth _____ and we went to _____ house.
                              (holiday)

The festivities included_____ and the tradition you liked the most

was_____

Our favorite memories of you are _____

_____

Your biggest accomplishment this year was _____

_____ at age _____

Drawn by _____ on _____

How You Grew

	48 inches							
42 inches								
36 inches								
30 inches								
24 inches								
18 inches								
12 inches								
	Birth	6 months	12 months	18 months	24 months	3 years	4 years	5 years

Afterword

Think back.... isn't there a picture book in your past which still makes you smile, and which brings you back to childhood days of discovery. Never is the power of pictures stronger than when a young child sits cradled within the circle of a grown-ups arms or when there is time to spend on hands and knees examining the details of a drawing. Looking at picture books is in a way like visiting a museum, and early picture book experiences will open your child's eyes to the appreciation of many kinds of art.

For these reasons, it is important to select the highest quality illustrations for your child. But with over 5,000 new children's books published each year, how is a parent to know which are worthy of your child's attention? Fortunately, we have the American Library Association to guide us. Each year since 1938, a committee of children's librarians has met to choose the "most distinguished American picture book for children." The artist of this book is awarded the Caldecott Medal, named after Randolph Caldecott, the nineteenth-century British illustrator of books for children. You will find Caldecott's illustrations for *Hey Diddle Diddle* on pages 36-37 of this book.

When your baby is a few months old, visit the Children's Room of your local library and ask for the librarian's help in selecting some well-illustrated collections of nursery rhymes. These are wonderful to chant aloud as you dress, feed and bathe your baby. When you find books that you enjoy and want to have as a part of your child's home library, visit your local bookstore. Your children's bookseller is also a specialist who is a valuable ally and will show you both classic and new picture books of high quality. The very simple board-books are the first ones for your baby to handle. In no time, you will be ready for your child's first visit to the museum to appreciate original art.

About the Contributors

The Department of Prints and Drawings of the Museum of Fine Arts, Boston has a large collection of illustrated books dating from the sixteenth century. For this book, we have chosen several examples from the turn of the century, a time often called "the golden age of children's book illustration."

Randolph Caldecott's (English, 1846-1886) work has delighted readers for over a century. He introduced the use of color wood engravings in children's books, an innovation which greatly influenced other illustrators for children's books. The major award for children's book illustration in the United States is named after him.

Walter Crane (English, 1845-1915) was a designer and artist who was influential in the Arts and Crafts Movement. He is remembered for his beautiful children's books, particularly *Triplets: The Baby's Opera, The Baby's Bouquet, The Baby's Own Aesop* (1899). He often drew a picture of a crane as a symbol of himself.

Richard Doyle (English, 1824-1883) began his career on the staff of the English humor magazine *Punch* and later devoted himself to illustrating children's stories. The wood engravings for *Fairyland (A Series of Pictures from the Elf World)* were inspired by William Allingham's poem *The Fairies*.

Kate Greenaway (English, 1846-1901) was an artist who was famous for her delicate and sentimental illustration of children dressed in eighteenth-century costume. Her book *A Apple Pie* was published in 1886.

Richard Kehl (b. 1936) is an American artist, teacher and author whose imaginative work has been exhibited in many countries. He created the back cover collage and interior decorations, which combine Victorian children's illustrations with beautiful floral art.

Eugene Field (American, 1850-1895) is often called the "poet of childhood." A Midwestern journalist, he is best remembered for his Dutch lullaby, "Wynken, Blynken and Nod."

The Enchanting Art on These Pages

Endpapers, title page and pages 6, 7 ,8, 16, 17, 42 and 43: Walter Crane (English, 1845-1915) from *Triplets: The Baby's Opera, The Baby's Bouquet, The Baby's Own Aesop* (London, George Routledge & Sons, 1899), Gift of Miss Ellen T. Bullard, 56.884.

Pages 18 and 19 and front cover: Kate Greenaway (English, 1846-1901) from *Alphabet* (London, George Routledge & Sons), Anonymous gift. Page 51: from *Under the Window,* Bequest of William A. Sargent, Book reg. 2356.

Page 20: Georges Lepape (French, 1887-1971) *"Chut!...Il dort." Robe d'interieur et manteau de Jeanne Lanvin; Gazette de Bon Ton,* Issue 6, Plate 25, Paris 1924; Gouache on paper; 6 1/2 x 5 1/4 inches; Library of the Department of Textiles;   DT TT500.

Pages 24, 25 and *64:* Maurice Boutet de Monvel (French, 1851-1913) from *Nos Enfants, Scènes de la Ville et des Champs* by Anatole France (Paris, Librarie Hatchette et Cie.,1900), Gift of Misses Aimée and Rosamond Lamb, 1970.258.

Pages 30, 31, 38, 39, 48 and 49: Richard Doyle (British, 1824-1883) from *Fairyland: Pictures from the Elf-World* (New York, D. Appleton & Co., 1870), Gift of Mrs. F. E. Donaldson Jr., 55.512.

Pages 36 and 37: Randolph Caldecott (British, 1846-1886) from *Hey Diddle Diddle Picture Book* (London, 1887), John H. and Ernestine A. Payne Fund, 55.1293.

Page 44: Anonymous (United States), "A Happy New Year," 1888, greeting card for Louis Prang, Gift of Wrightson Christopher, 1989.

Page 44: Jessie Wilcox Smith (American, 1863-1935), "Natural History," from *Rhymes of Real Children* by Betty Sage (New York, Duffield and Company, 1913), Anonymous gift.

Page 45: Anonymous (English) greeting card for Raphael Tuck & Sons, Gift of Wrightson Christopher, 1989.

The Man in the Moon looked
Out of the moon,
Looked out of the moon
and said,
'Tis time for all children
on the earth
To think about getting to bed!'

The End